21st **Century Skills INNOVATION LIBRARY**

UNOFFICIAL
GUIDES

AMONG US:
Beginner's Guide

T0062040

CHERRY LAKE PUBLISHING • ANN ARBOR, MICHIGAN

by Josh Gregory

Cherry Lake Press

Published in the United States of America by Cherry Lake Publishing
Ann Arbor, Michigan
www.cherrylakepublishing.com

Reading Adviser: Beth Walker Gambro, MS, Ed., Reading Consultant, Yorkville, IL
Photo Credits: ©Jarretera/Shutterstock, cover and page 1

Cherry Lake Press is an imprint of Cherry Lake Publishing Group

Library of Congress Cataloging-in-Publication Data has been filed and is available
at catalog.loc.gov

Cherry Lake Publishing Group would like to acknowledge the work of the Part-
nership for 21st Century Learning, a Network of Battelle for Kids. Please visit
http://www.batelleforkids.org/networks/p21 for more information.

Printed in the United States of America
Corporate Graphics

Contents

Chapter 1

A Streaming Success Story

One of the biggest hit video games of 2020 wasn't created by a well-known company. It didn't have a big budget and it wasn't part of a famous series. In fact, it wasn't even a new release!

TOTAL TASKS COMPLETED

Ping: 62 ms

Admin: Enter Id Code
Storage: Fix Wiring (0/3)
Reactor: Divert Power to Office (0/2)
Greenhouse: Clean O2 Filter
Reactor: Unlock Manifolds
Admin: Prime Shields
Oxygen Depleted in 42 (0/2)

Tasks

ea

CL

Nanis

Among Us may not have the fanciest graphics compared to other games, but it is just as fun to play.

Back in June 2018, a small team of **developers** called Innersloth released a game called *Among Us* on the iOS and Android app stores. Innersloth had only worked on a couple of games before. Few people took notice of their latest release. At any given moment, you could find only a handful of people in the entire world who were playing the game online.

The idea for *Among Us* was based on social **deduction** games such as *Werewolf* and *Mafia*. People have played these kinds of games in person for decades. Typically, a group of players works to figure out which of the other players are secretly enemies. The enemy players must lie and keep the rest of the players from discovering them. There are social deduction board games, card games, and even video games. When they started designing *Among Us*, the developers at Innersloth originally planned for their version to be an in-person game played using mobile devices. However, they eventually realized that it could work just as well when played online.

Even though *Among Us* wasn't a smash hit right away, Innersloth kept working on it. They knew the basic idea of the game was good. They just needed

Enrique was not An Impostor.

a way to get the word out. With a team of just three people and little extra money, they didn't have many resources to rely on. And even though it's possible for unknown people to gain fame and influence using social media, succeeding this way is often easier said than done. "We're really bad at **marketing**," Innersloth's Marcus Bromander said in a 2020 interview. Many game developers work with professional marketers to advertise their creations. But for a team as small as Innersloth, that simply wasn't an option.

Innersloth continued doing what they know how to do best: working on games. Little by little, they added new features and fixed **bugs** in *Among Us*. In November 2018, they released a PC version of the game on Steam. They hoped this would help *Among Us* catch on with a wider audience. Every so often, Innersloth would notice a boost in the numbers. "We stuck with *Among Us* a lot longer than we probably should have from a pure business standpoint," Innersloth's Forest Willard said in an interview in 2020. "We tried to quit and should have quit several times."

Eventually they reached a point where a few thousand players might be online at any moment. Thanks to a couple of successful streamers, the game found an audience in places such as Brazil and South Korea. "I feel like every time we saw big waves of players, that pushed us to get excited and want to do more with it," Bromander said. The team put in long hours to improve the game. They created new levels and made the game run more smoothly. But by the start of 2020, they were almost ready to move on and try starting a new project.

In July 2020, two full years after *Among Us* was first released, everything changed almost overnight. That month, an extremely popular Twitch streamer called Sodapoppin began going live with *Among Us*. Millions of viewers followed Sodapoppin's channel, and they all got to see how fun *Among Us* could be. It was a better advertisement than the team at Innersloth could ever have created on their own.

Over the following couple of months, *Among Us* rocketed to the top of the Twitch charts. Some of the most popular streamers on the service joined in,

Levels such as MIRA HQ were not available in the earliest versions of *Among Us*.

Winning regularly requires strategy, careful thinking, and the ability to figure out when someone is lying.

creating even more buzz around the game. Many viewers were encouraged to try the game for themselves. By the end of September 2020, *Among Us* had been downloaded more than 100 million times. At peak times, millions of people were playing online at once. Across social media, fans shared *Among Us* memes, songs, and more. *Among Us* had officially gone from a little-known underdog to one of the most popular games on the planet.

Many video game fans noted a possible reason that players had connected to *Among Us* so suddenly:

Famous Fans

Among Us has gotten so famous that it has sometimes drawn attention from unexpected places. Headlines in major newspapers covered the game's unbelievable rise in 2020. Some of the biggest influencers on Twitch and TikTok flocked to the game. Believe it or not, even members of the U.S. Congress joined in on the fun. On October 20, 2020, Congresswomen Alexandria Ocasio-Cortez and Ilhan Omar logged on to Twitch to play *Among Us* and chat with viewers about the 2020 elections. Big-name Twitch celebrities such as Pokimane and DrLupo participated as well, playing in matches with the U.S. Representatives. Together, they drew hundreds of thousands of viewers, making it one of the most-watched Twitch streams in history.

the COVID-19 **pandemic**. Stuck inside and unable to hang out in person, many people were looking for new ways to have fun with friends online. *Among Us* was the perfect solution to this problem. Groups of friends could easily gather online and play casually for hours as they chatted.

The rapid rise of *Among Us* caught the developers at Innersloth off guard. At first, they weren't quite sure how to handle it. In August 2020, they announced that they were going to make a sequel to their suddenly successful game. But they canceled these plans almost

Unlike many video games, *Among Us* requires a lot of talking and communicating with fellow players.

immediately. Instead, they decided to keep adding to the original game and making it even better. This type of plan has worked very well for other popular online games such as *Fortnite* and *Minecraft*. These games have remained at the top of the charts for years without ever receiving sequels. However, they look much different today than they did when they were first released. *Among Us* is only going to get better as time goes on. Now is the perfect time to dive in!

Chapter 2

Jumping In

It's very easy to get started with *Among Us*. All you need is an iOS or Android mobile device or a Windows PC. The game does not require the latest device or most powerful computer. Because it is somewhat old and has simple graphics, it will run on just about anything. If you're playing on a mobile device the game is completely free. On PC, you can download it

The main menu of *Among Us* offers just a few options to choose from.

through Steam or itch.io for about $5. After *Among Us* became a huge hit, Innersloth also started working on console versions of the game. The Nintendo Switch version was released in December 2020. Like the PC version, it is a $5 download.

There are several options on the main menu. The "Local" option will let you set up a game with other players connected to the same Wi-Fi network. Each player will need their own device to join the game. Back at the main menu, choose the "Online" option to play online with people anywhere in the world. Select "Host" if you want to set up a game for other players to join. This will allow you to set some of the basic rules of the match, such as how many players will participate and which level you will play on. Select "Public" if you want to find a random game with strangers. You'll then get a list of available matches to choose from. The "Private" option will let you join a game hosted by a friend. Your friend will have to share a code that you enter before joining. This lets you enjoy private matches with friends. Strangers won't be able to join in if they don't have your code.

A match of *Among Us* can have anywhere from 4 to 10 players. At the start of each match, 1 to 3 of

Protect Your Privacy

Among Us is most fun when you're playing with people you know well. After all, being able to tell when someone is lying or acting strange is a big part of the game. The in-game discussions work best when you can do them over voice chat or in person. *Among Us* does not have a built-in voice chat system. You'll need to chat with friends using phone calls, Discord, or however else you like to keep in touch. If you want to chat inside the game itself, you'll have to type out your messages or use quick chat.

Sometimes you might not have enough friends around for a full match. In these cases, you'll find yourself playing with random players online. This is perfectly fine. However, you should always remember to be careful when communicating online with people you don't know in real life. Don't reveal personal information such as your real name, where you live, or where you go to school. Instead, stick to chatting about the game. If another player is making you uncomfortable, quit the game and tell a trusted adult.

the players will be randomly chosen to be Impostors. The rest will be Crewmates. Crewmates will not know which players are Impostors. They will only be told how many Impostors there are. Impostors, on the other hand, will know who the other Impostors are.

If you are a Crewmate, your job during the match will be to complete the list of tasks seen in the upper left corner of your screen. Each task takes place in

Crewmate

There is 1 Impostor among us

You'll know from the beginning of a match how many Impostors you need to deal with.

a different part of the level and requires players to complete a short mini-game. As you work on your tasks, you'll also need to try and figure out who the Impostors are. Impostors look and move around just like Crewmates. However, instead of completing tasks, their goal is to eliminate the Crewmates one by one without getting caught. Crewmates will win a match if they complete all of their tasks or discover all the Impostors. Impostors will win if they eliminate enough Crewmates to leave an equal number on both teams. In other words, if there are two Impostors, they will win once there are only two Crewmates remaining. If there are three Impostors, they will win once there are only three Crewmates.

When an Impostor attacks a Crewmate, the Crewmate's body falls to the ground. If another Crewmate sees the attack or finds the body, they can call a meeting. The game pauses, and the players can hold a discussion and try to figure out who the **culprit** is. This is where the game gets really interesting. Impostors can bluff and pretend they are regular Crewmates. Meanwhile, Crewmates have to convince each other of which other players they think are Impostors. At the end of the discussion, all of the players vote on who they think the Impostor is. The player who loses the vote is eliminated from the match, no matter whether they were truly an Impostor or actually just a Crewmate.

At the start of each match, all of the players will be gathered in a small room together. Here, you can use the computer to customize your appearance. You can change your character's color, as long as another player is not using the same one. You can also choose a hat, a pet, and a skin. Hats are exactly what they sound like: decorative objects your character

Custom Settings
Map: The Skeld
Impostors: 2
Confirm Ejects: On
Emergency Meetings:
Anonymous Votes: Off
Emergency Cooldown: 20s
Discussion Time: 30s
Voting Time: 45s
Player Speed: 2x
Crewmate Vision: 5x
Impostor Vision: 2.5x
Kill Cooldown: 15s
Kill Distance: Long
Task Bar Updates: Always
Visual Tasks: On
Common Tasks: 2
Long Tasks: 2
Short Tasks: 2

Ping: 50

Color   Hat   Pet   Skin   Game

Feel free to change your character's appearance as often as you like. It doesn't affect anything about the game other than looks.

can wear on their head. Pets are small creatures that will follow your character around. Skins are different clothing your character can wear. You'll start out with a few different hats and skins to choose from. If you want more choices or to add a pet, you'll have to purchase them from the in-game store. You can do this by clicking the dollar-sign button in the character customization screen. Each item costs a couple of dollars. All of them are purely for looks. They do not give you any advantages in the game.

Chapter 3

Trust and Teamwork

Because there are always more Crewmates than Impostors, you will likely play most matches as a Crewmate. This means you'll need to get good at completing tasks if you want to succeed.

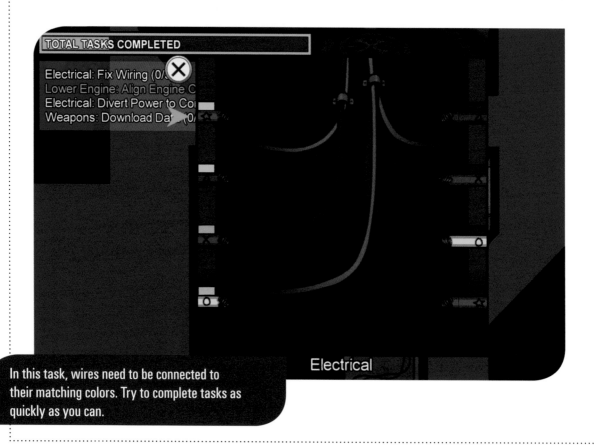

TOTAL TASKS COMPLETED

Electrical: Fix Wiring (0/
Lower Engine: Align Engine C
Electrical: Divert Power to Cor
Weapons: Download Da (0/

Electrical

In this task, wires need to be connected to their matching colors. Try to complete tasks as quickly as you can.

Want a chance to explore and try out all of the different tasks without the pressure of a real match? Select "Freeplay" from the main menu. You can then choose which level you want to play. You'll be dropped into an empty version of the level with no other players. Now you can wander around as long as you like and learn where the different rooms are.

In Freeplay, you'll see a computer near your starting point. Click on it to select which tasks you want to try. They are organized by which rooms they take place in. You can also use this computer to switch back and forth from being a Crewmate and an Impostor. Spend as much time as you like learning and practicing. Then you can test your skills in a real match!

There are several different kinds of tasks to complete. Some are simple puzzles, while others are based on timing. They can be grouped into a few categories. Short tasks are those that can be completed quickly in a single step. Long tasks might have multiple steps or require you to wait around in one place for a certain amount of time. Each Crewmate will have a different set of short and long tasks to complete in each round of the game. Their lists will also contain common tasks. These are tasks that are the same for every Crewmate in the game.

Each task has to be done in a certain room on the map. This will be clearly labeled on your task list.

For example, one list item might say "Admin: Swipe Card." This means you need to complete the Swipe Card task in the Admin room. To see where different rooms are, click on the map icon in the upper right corner of your screen. This will place a large map on top of the screen. It will show the names of the map's rooms, your location, and the locations of your tasks. If you want, you can leave the map up as you move around. It will make it a little hard to see what is going on, but it can also help you **navigate** easier.

There are several different levels in *Among Us*. Each one has a different layout and different sets of possible tasks. You'll need to learn how all of them work if you want to play the game well. As you work through your tasks, you need to keep an eye on the other players. You should always be on the lookout for hints that they might be Impostors or solid proof that they are Crewmates.

Some tasks are visual tasks. As you complete these, your character will perform an animation that shows they are doing the task. Other players will be able to see it if they are nearby. When completing

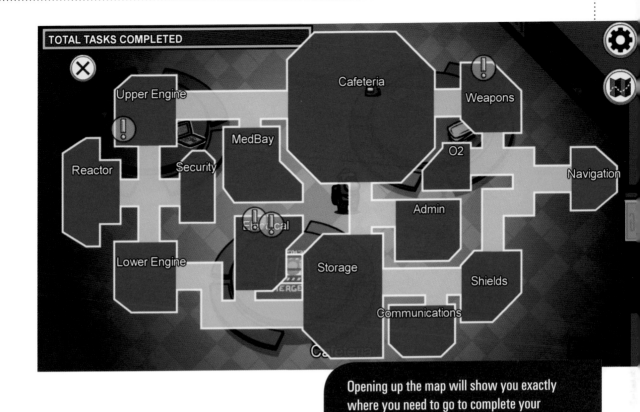

TOTAL TASKS COMPLETED

Upper Engine

Cafeteria

Weapons

MedBay

O2

Reactor

Security

Navigation

Admin

Electrical

Lower Engine

Storage

Shields

Communications

Opening up the map will show you exactly where you need to go to complete your assigned tasks.

nonvisual tasks, it will just look like your character is standing there. If you see someone complete a visual task, it means they are definitely a Crewmate. This is because Impostors cannot actually complete tasks.

If you spot one player attacking another, you have definitely found an Impostor. Similarly, you might see a player leave a room. When you go into that room, you find another player's body. This is evidence that the player you saw leaving the room could be an Impostor.

Impostors can also use vents to quickly move from one room to another. If you see a player go into or pop out of a vent, they are definitely an Impostor.

If you discover a body or spot someone behaving suspiciously (or as many players say, "sus"), you can call a meeting. Calmly explain what you saw and where it happened. Don't make accusations or call meetings without evidence. It will only hurt your chances if you end up voting out a fellow Crewmate by mistake. If another player calls the meeting, listen to what they have to say. Is the argument convincing?

When you see this screen, you know something big has happened. Time to talk!

TOTAL TASKS COMPLETED

You're dead. Finish your tasks to win.
Electrical: Fix Wiring (0/3)
Reactor: Start Reactor
Electrical: Divert Power to Lower Engine (0/2)
Electrical: Calibrate Distributor

Tasks

CL

Ping: 50 ms

Your character will have a slightly different appearance after becoming a ghost.

If you aren't sure, you can always choose to skip your vote. If enough players skip voting, no one will be kicked out during the meeting.

If an Impostor knocks you out, you'll become a ghost. Ghosts can only talk to other ghosts, and they can't call meetings or report bodies. This keeps them from revealing who attacked them. However, they can still move around and complete tasks. In other words, you can still help your team win, so don't give up!

Chapter 4

Stop Looking Sus

When playing as an Impostor, your number one goal is to blend in and avoid detection. The best way to do this is to avoid doing anything suspicious in front of a Crewmate. For example, don't attack anyone or use a vent unless you are out of sight. You should also watch out for security cameras. Crewmates can check these cameras from the security room. If they are looking at a camera, it will light

Players looking through security cameras will get a view like this, letting them see several parts of the level at once.

Sabotage and kill everyone.
Fake Tasks:
Admin: Swipe Card
Weapons: Clear Asteroids (0/20)
Electrical: Divert Power to O2 (0/2)
Electrical: Calibrate Distributor

Tasks

CL

To fake a task, simply stand close to the panel you would normally click on to start the task.

up. Don't do anything wrong when you are near a lit camera!

To blend in better, you can fake doing tasks. Simply go to the location where a task is done and stand nearby. You'll even get a handy list of tasks to fake in the upper left corner of the screen. As you move around the map, try to keep track of where other players are and where they're headed.

When the time is right, go ahead and attack another player. You will instantly knock them out. Be careful, though. Each time you attack, you'll need to wait a while before you do it again. This means you can't attack multiple players one after the other. Before attacking, have a plan in place to avoid getting caught. For example, you can quickly jump into a nearby vent or simply run away. When you do, make sure no one sees you running from the body. And whatever you do, don't let anyone see you using a vent! It's an immediate giveaway that you are an Impostor.

Another strategy is to attack someone and then immediately report the body yourself. If you are good

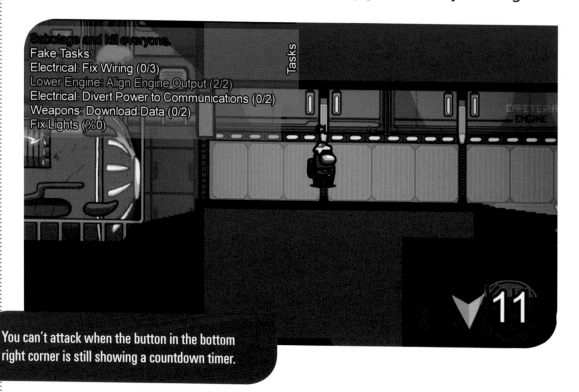

You can't attack when the button in the bottom right corner is still showing a countdown timer.

Going Forward

There are big things in store for *Among Us* in the future. Innersloth is working on bringing the game to as many different gaming systems as possible. This will allow even more players to join in the fun. The developers are also working on new levels, tasks, and other features. In other words, there shouldn't be any reason to get bored of the game for quite a while.

Innersloth is also working to add an account system and friend list, much like you'd find in other games. Because their team is so small and *Among Us* started as a mobile game, these features weren't built in from the start. Once they are added, it will be much easier for players to see if their friends are online and find out if they want to play.

at bluffing, you can convince the other players that you found the body and saw someone else in the room. You'll end up looking like a good Crewmate, and another player will get the blame. Similarly, you might be in a meeting and notice that one Crewmate is mistakenly accusing another Crewmate. Join in and agree, and you might be able to easily get rid of another Crewmate!

As an Impostor, you also have the ability to perform **sabotage**. Tap the sabotage button in the bottom right corner of the screen to get started. From there, you can choose between a number of problems you can cause for the Crewmates. For example, you can cause a Reactor Meltdown. This will start a timer, and two Crewmates will have to rush to the reactor room and fix the problem before time runs out. If they fail, the Impostors will automatically win the round! Other forms of sabotage include locking doors and turning out the lights. Only one sabotage can be used at a time, so you can't just keep making life hard for the Crewmates. But if you time your sabotage right, it will give you an opportunity to attack.

If you get discovered and voted out, you can still help the other Impostors win. You can't attack or use the vents anymore, but you can still sabotage. You can also float through walls, making it easy to zoom around the map.

Once you play a few rounds, you should have a feel for the basics of *Among Us*. However, every match can have surprising moments, no matter how many times you've played before. Every individual player has their own style. Seeing how different people try to bluff and make arguments is half the fun of the game.

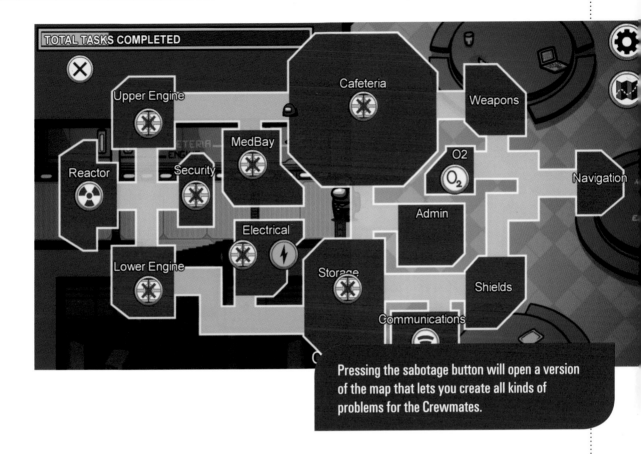

TOTAL TASKS COMPLETED

Upper Engine

Cafeteria

Weapons

MedBay

O2

Navigation

Reactor

Security

Admin

Electrical

Lower Engine

Storage

Shields

Communications

Pressing the sabotage button will open a version of the map that lets you create all kinds of problems for the Crewmates.

It's a great way to hang out with friends and make new ones. Don't worry if your team doesn't win every round. Just focus on having a good time!

Glossary

bugs (BUHGS) errors in a computer program's code that cause the program to do something unexpected

culprit (KUHL-prit) someone who is guilty of something

deduction (deh-DUK-shuhn) the process of figuring something out through careful reasoning

developers (dih-VEL-uh-purz) people who make video games or other computer programs

marketing (MAR-kih-ting) the process of advertising and selling something

navigate (NAV-uh-gayt) to make your way from one place to another

pandemic (pan-DEM-ik) a widespread outbreak of illness

sabotage (SAB-uh-tahj) to deliberately cause something to malfunction

Find Out More

BOOKS

Cunningham, Kevin. *Video Game Designer*. Ann Arbor, MI: Cherry Lake Publishing, 2016.

Loh-Hagan, Virginia. *Video Games*. Ann Arbor, MI: Cherry Lake Publishing, 2021.

Powell, Marie. *Asking Questions About Video Games*. Ann Arbor, MI: Cherry Lake Publishing, 2016.

WEBSITES

Among Us
https://innersloth.com/gameAmongUs.php
Check out Innersloth's official *Among Us* site for the latest updates on the game's development.

Among Us Wiki
https://among-us.fandom.com/wiki/Among_Us_Wiki
This fan-created site is packed with info about every detail of *Among Us*.

Index

About the Author

Josh Gregory is the author of more than 150 books for kids. He has written about everything from animals to technology to history. A graduate of the University of Missouri–Columbia, he currently lives in Chicago, Illinois.